PICTURE WINDOW

A CAROL LYNN PEARSON
～ COLLECTION ～

From Beginnings to the Present

GOLD LEAF PRESS

Picture Window
© 1996 by Carol Lynn Pearson
All rights reserved.
Printed in the United States

No portion of this book may be reproduced in any form without written
from the publisher, Gold Leaf Press, 2533 North Carson St., Suite 1544,
Carson City, NV 89706

Library of Congress Cataloging-in-Publication Data

Pearson, Carol Lynn.
Picture window : a Carol Lynn Pearson collection :
from Beginnings to the present.
p. cm.
Includes index.
ISBN 1-882723-27-9
I. Title
PS3566.E227P53 1996
811'.54--dc20   965449
CIP

10 9 8 7 6 5 4 3 2 1

CONTENTS

PREFACE

Early on in my writing career I felt it was terribly unfair that those who read my books know much more about me than I know about them. Who in the world are these people who are lining up to buy my *Beginnings*, I wondered.

And then I began to get little glimpses from letters, phone calls, visits. I know my readers now. You're the woman who called to tell me about her own painful "Trial Number Five," saying "I guess we just keep on trying, don't we?" You're the older woman who sat in tears as I read "Millie's Mother's Red Dress" and then embraced me, saying, "That was me! That was me!" You're the man who told me he saw himself in "The Steward" and afterwards treated his wife a little bit differently. You're the young mother of three small children who grabbed me just the other day at church and said that life was a little easier if she kept one of my books by her bed. You're the serviceman who told me he had hand-copied my whole book of love poems and was sending it page by page to his sweetheart back home because it said everything he wanted to say to her.

I know who you are now, not only because of the letters and the calls but because I know now more and more who I am. And believing, as Matthew Arnold wrote, that "The same heart beats in every human breast" and, as I once wrote, "Divided by darkness, blended by sun—by some amazing miracle, we come out one," I feel I know you quite well. And I reverence you. And I am grateful that we are sharing life's wonderful journey together.

OUR DIVINE JOURNEY

Beginnings

Today
You came running
With a small specked egg
Warm in your hand.
You could barely understand
I know
As I told you
Of Beginnings—
Of egg and bird;
Told, too,
That years ago
You began
Smaller than sight.
And then
As egg yearns for sky
And seed
Stretches to tree
You became
Like me.

Oh
But there's
So much more.
You and I,
Child,
Have just begun.

Think:
Worlds from now
What might we be—
We
Who are seed
Of Deity.

Optical Illusion

Time is a stage magician
Pulling sleight-of-hand tricks
To make you think things go.

There
Eclipsed by the quick scarf
A lifetime of loves.

Zip—
The child is man.
Zip—
The friend in your arms
Is earth.
Zip—
The green tree is gold, is white,
Is smoking ash, is gone.

Zip—
Time's trick goes on.
All things loved—
Now you see them, now you don't.

Oh, this world has more
Of coming and of going
Than I can bear.
I guess it's eternity I want,
Where all things are
And always will be,
Where I can hold my loves
A little looser,
Where finally we realize
Time
Is the only thing that really dies.

Creation Continued

I will continue
To create the universe today
Right where God left off.

Little pockets of chaos
Somehow survived the ordering
And I feel moved
To move upon them
As in the beginning
The Spirit of God moved
Upon the face of the waters.

I will move upon my backyard today
And the weeds will be subdued
And the flowers can grow
And it will be good.

I will move long-distance
Upon a broken heart
And leave a little balm
And it will be good.

I will move upon
The hunger of my children
With salad and spaghetti
Which is Emily's favorite
And it will be good
And even they will say so.
And I will move too
Upon their minds
Leaving a little poem
Or an important thought
And that will be even better
Though they won't say so.

I will move upon
Birth defects and cancer
With five and ten dollar checks
To help the scientists
Who are battling the big chaos
And I will move upon world hunger
With a twenty-four dollar check
For little Marilza in Brazil
And it will be good.

I will move upon
The kitchen floor
And the dirty laundry
And a blank piece of paper
And at the end of the day
Have a little creation to show.

And the evening and the morning
Are my eighteen thousand
And ninety-sixth day
And tomorrow will start another one.
And here is chaos and there is chaos
And who knows if creation
Will finally be done?

The Cast

I lost the starring part in "Our Town"
To Linda, a girl not half as good as me,
Who kept her eyes down
For the whole tryout, and even stuttered.

When the cast was posted
And the high school drama coach
Saw me reading it through my tears,
He put an arm around me and said,
"Now, look—things are not always as they appear.
This is not Broadway;
It's an educational institution.
We're here for two reasons—to put on a show,
And, more important, to help people grow.
Someday you'll see."

So Linda played Emily,
And she didn't even stutter.
And I was Third Woman at the Wedding,
Watching and wondering how he knew
What she could really do
If she had the chance.

Since then I have guessed that God,
Being a whole lot smarter
Than my high school drama coach,
Might be offstage sometimes
With an arm around a questioning cast:
"Now, don't try to outguess me.
Sometimes the first shall be last
And the last shall be first.
Mortality is an educational institution.
We've got to put on the show,
And, too, we've got to help people grow."

As I walk through the scenes
Watch the costumes move and listen to the lines
Of the powerful, the weak, the rich, the poor,
I look at the leads with less awe than most,
And at the spear-carriers with more.

Of the Mysteries

I know only as much of God and the world
As a creature with two eyes must;
But what I do understand, I love
And what I don't understand, I trust.

Earth-Bound

That look on a little face
As a kite breaks loose
As higher and higher
It floats and flaps—

That look,
Is it sadness for loss
Or envy perhaps?

Tug at your own string,
Little one.
When the wind is right
You will snap toward the sun.

Urgent to Marilyn

Marilyn had a job—
Working out her salvation.
It wasn't nine to five.
It was nine to nine
In twenty-four-hour shifts.

And there was no vacation,
And in case she should get fired
Nobody else was hiring,
So Marilyn worked hard
And she worked fast
And she worked in fear.

The boss was away a lot
And Marilyn wondered
If he liked her work,
And not knowing, she worked harder.
She did everything on every list
Twice over to make sure.

She didn't have much fun
On the job.
It was more the retirement
Benefits she was there for,
The mansion, the glory.

On a typical day
She ran frantically from
The school committee chairperson department
To the carpool department
To the physical fitness
Department.

She even stopped running
Past the yoga and meditation department

And sat long enough
To cross that off her list.

And then she ran
To the home beautification department
Ran with scriptures on cassette in one hand
And self-help in the other.

Ran because there were
Twenty-two minutes left to fill,
Ran past the boss's memo
On the bulletin board:

"Urgent to Marilyn:
Peace, be still."

Real Tears

When I played Joan of Arc
I cried real tears.

"Help me, Joan,"
Said the Bishop of Beauvais,
"I do not wish to burn you!"

That's when the tears would come,
Real tears on cue
Every night for four nights.

When we struck the set
I saw them,
Little dry drops on the black canvas.
Strange, I couldn't feel a thing now,
But there they were.

I believe it will be
A little like that
When the current show closes.
When the set is struck
And the costumes cleared away,
I may drop by with a friend and say,

"Look—when I was playing Carol Lynn,
Back in space and in years,
There is the spot,
The very spot,
Where I cried real tears."

The Lesson

Yes, my fretting
Frowning child,
I could cross
The room to you
More easily.
But I've already
Learned to walk
So I make you
Come to me.

Let go, now—
There!
You see?

Oh, remember
This simple lesson,
Child,
And when
In later years
You cry out
With tight fists
And tears
"Oh, help me,
God—please"
Just listen
And you'll hear
A silent voice:

"I would, child,
I would.
But I know
It's you, not I,
Who needs to grow."

The Light

There is
A fire that filters
Down the night
Of this world—
A light-line
Sparked by God
In human lanterns.
I watch them
And my way clears.

But here
One flickers
Then fails,
And farther off
Another's glow
Guides only the
Largest steps.

Still I can see
For God also kindled
(And gently blows
To brighten)
A flame
In me.

Within

I read a map once
Saying the kingdom of God
Was within me
But I never trusted
Such unlikely ground.

I went out.
I scoured schools
And libraries
And chapels and temples
And other people's eyes
And the skies and the rocks,
And I found treasures
From the kingdom's treasury
But not the kingdom.

Finally
I came in quiet
For a rest
And turned on the light.

And there
Just like a surprise party
Was all the smiling royalty,
King, Queen, court.

People have been
Locked up for less, I know.
But I tell you
Something marvelous
Is bordered by this skin:

I am a castle
And the kingdom of God
Is within.

Prayer at Table

The food, yes—
But most of all
Bless
Me.
The bread is
Full and good
As I would be.
Oh, Lord,
My only leaven,
Work
Warm me
Let me lift
Toward heaven.

Provision for the End

What to do when
The dawn brings night
And the moon spins out
And the stars fall white?

Wait calm in the silence
The black sky spilled:
Your lamp will light—
If it is filled.

Perspective from Mortality

My life is patterned as the palm
Of a rain-washed leaf, calm
Cut and full.
But
I view my life from underneath
Which—like the patterned leaf—
Is fuzzed and dull.

Lament of a Grouch

I knew
That in heaven
All are happy.
But I wish
I'd known
The reason
Before:

Only
To the happy
Do they
Open the door.

The Eleventh Hour

Had I been born
To other centuries—
How pleasant
To stretch
In the sun
And choose from
All life's
Possibilities
This one
Or that.
To prove the Earth is round
Or tame the ocean,
To write a dictionary
Or expound
On Shakespeare's
Subtle irony.

But these are
Daytime jobs.
And
As I was born
To time's
Saturday night
My ordained task
Is to kindle
The Sabbath light.

The Family of Light

Kindled into the family
That sparked the sun
We came—
With suns and moons and stars
In us forever.

And the Mother
Who nurtures new light
In the warmest of all wombs,
And the Father
Who holds in His hands
The growing glow and blows it brighter—
Together placed us in another room.

It is dark here.
Deep within element
We dim and dim.
And to slim the ray
That might find its way out
We handcraft clever bushels
Of modest, fashionable fears.

But long darkness is untenable
And we yearn for the burning
To begin again.

We have had too much night.
Shall we—
Shall we together shed our bushels
And stand revealed—
Sons and daughters of light?

GOD AND ETERNITY

The Measure

Friend,
Do you measure land
With a barometer?
Can you understand
The law of gravity
By testing
The freezing point of mud
At its greatest density?

There is no God
By knowledge's rules?
Friend,
Examine your tools.

To discover God
You must form your plan
To the nature
Of God
Not the nature of man.
The only key
Is that forgotten faculty
That pulses through you
Now and then
Eluding the hand
And startling the mind.
Spirit, it's called.

Friend,
You will not find
God through mistaken tools.
Who weighs a stone
With a measuring tape?
Fools.

Unpinned

I hope that humans
Never pin down
Love or God.

Things pinned down
(Like butterflies)
Lose something
(Like life).

I can go with progress.
I am grateful
For a long life span
For medicine and computers
And I'm glad to know
The layout of the
Galaxy.

But let some
Mysteries win.

Let love and God be free
As a million monarchs
To touch our faces
With bright wings
And leave wonder in our eyes
As they rise
From the hand-held pin.

The Beneficiary

I was not there.
But they say
It happened for me.
On the cross it happened
And in the tomb.
For me—
Vicariously.

But how?
It was His sacrifice
Not mine.
It was He who wept
Who bled
Not me.

Except—
Why, look—
At the flick of a finger
I instantly receive
What Edison
Gave his full life
To achieve.

Perhaps
If one man
Searching the skies
Willed us the key
To conquer night—
May not another
A greater
Bequeath from the cross
The key to
Eternal light?

The Watchers

There is a tomb
In old Jerusalem
Where one is told
Christ spent
Death's interim,
And many walk
That way
In curiosity.

"Three days
Behind the stone,"
He said,
"And then
A longer time
In heaven before
I come again."

But few
There are
Who watch
That door.

Earth-Soul

The earth
Has a soul—
I know.
How else came
The sorry groans
That heaved
A rush of
Fire and wind
And blood and
Crashing stones?

She felt the
Sad procession
Climb the hill—
She heard
The nails—
She knew.
And with the
Bursting
Of the heart
Upon the cross
Her heart burst
Too.

The Offering

For ancient wrongs
God required
The burning of flesh
An offering fresh
From the flocks.

But Christ turned
The outside in.
And for my sin
God demands
The harder part:
No yearling lamb
On the altar
But my own
Wounded heart.

Bethlehem

My pilgrimage to Bethlehem
Was by bus.
I shared my seat
With a crate of irreverent hens
And breathed air bruised by Eastern cigarettes.
I envied the clean, green walk of the shepherds.

At the bus stop I looked
For the familiar village of my books.
Boys with toy rifles ran
From little yellowed houses
Up rocky hills playing kill the Jews.

"Guide?" asked a man
At the Church of the Nativity.
"Thank you, no, I can't pay a guide."
"No charge. Please. Is free."

He showed me the place
Where they say the birth was
Down underneath the stairs.
I breathed for hay
And listened for the lambs.
But the sputtering of perfumed wax
Got in my way
And the Latin chanting from the church above
And my guide proudly pointing out
Which sect owned which part
Of the ornamented, golden altar.
"Beautiful, no?"
"Yes. Lovely."

We stepped out of the church
Into his small shop.
"Here you buy souvenir of Bethlehem.
Very nice. Very cheap."

Waiting for the bus to leave
I fingered my small New Testament
With its carved cover
And my two salad sets of olive wood.
The boys ran by with their rifles
And a radio rocked out The Beatles.

Oh, Bethlehem was better in my dreams.

The sky was darkening when the bus
Lurched its return to the city.

There—above the hill—one star,
One tiny, bright, honest-to-heaven star.
I turned the pages of my new souvenir.

Heaven and earth shall pass away . . .
But I am the same,
Yesterday, today, and forever.

I leaned back, listened to the lambs
And smelled the hay.

Nativity Scene

Touch the tiny Jesus gently now—
Put him in the bed.
No, dear, I don't know why the wise man
Wears a turban on his head.
That's just the way they dressed.
Be careful with the lamb—it's best
To hold him with both hands.
It's late in Bethlehem—
That's why the star shines bright.
It showed the wise men where to come.

No, dear, the star can't really shine.
It's wood—it's just pretend.
But last night,
The star we wished on, high above the moon—
That was real. Remember?

The lamb won't bleat, dear.
Even when you're asleep.
It's a sort of clay. But you did hear
Your uncle's sheep
Calling in alarm
Through the midnight of a snow-filled farm?

The baby Jesus
Clay.
But listen, dear (put down the lamb)—
I've a promise for you,
A promise God will keep:
As you've seen stars
And as you've heard the sheep
One day you'll know and hear and see
This Jesus too,
In reality.

The Reason

A certain panic
Finds me
When I see
A forest, a train
A library.
So many trees to touch
Places
Faces yet to view
And, too
So many words to read.

If I concede
All space to earth
All time to life
The disproportion
Is absurd
(My tiny taste
And the giant waste
Of all creation
I've not known).
What a wretched
Faithless view
Of God's economy.

It isn't true.
The forest, the train
The library—
Are why we have
Eternity.

A Heavenly Message to One Who Has Never Had a Single Visionary Experience

It's not that I have
Nothing to say to you—
It's just that I never shout
When a whisper will do.

Milk before Meat

Why worry on
Exactly how
A body will arise
Once someone dies?

I can't even
Understand
The manifest things—
Like how
A seagull flies
From merely
Having wings.

To an Atheist

God must have a huge sense of humor
So righteously to resist
The temptation of turning the tables
On your pretending He does not exist.

To a Beloved Skeptic

I cannot talk with you of God
Since sober wise you grew;
So my one recourse in charity
Is to talk with God of you.

The Source

If God is love
The source
The spring
Should not the lover
Pilgrimage there—
Reverently
Seeking supply?—

That the cup he gives
Will not be dry.

PRAYER

Affirmation

Some
Heaven-sought answers
Come in sound—
A voice perhaps—
But I have found
Mine always come
In utter silence.

My heart
A swollen sea
Stops tearing
At its shores
And gradually stills.

The whipping
Of the wind
The gull's sharp cry—
All sounds
Cease.

I listen
To the answer.

Silence
Speaks clearly:
It speaks peace.

The Uses of Prayer

Heaven
Holds out the blessing
Like a bright
Ripe fruit
Only waiting
For us to ask it:

Our words
Weave the basket.

Prayer

This radio set
Called prayer
Is designed
For remarkably
Simple repair.
When the lines fail
There is no doubt
Which half
Of the set
Is out.

Martyr's Prayer

Dear God,
I would not turn
From the test of fire.
No flame burns
So hot that
I would leave Thee.

But often
At weary bedtime
I cannot hold
My knees to the floor—
So cold
So very cold.

The Proficient Prayer

I'm getting very
Proficient at praying
I will admit.

I give the prayer
And I answer it.

Guilt

I have no vulture sins, God
That overhang my sky
To climb, grey-feathering the air
And swoop carnivorously.

It's just the tiny sins, God
That from memory appear
Like tedious, buzzing flies to dart
Like static through my prayer.

The Late Afternoon Prayer of Clara Louise

So, Heavenly Father,
You've got to do something.
You know I don't bother you
Except when I'm desperate.
And I am—I just can't—

Crying out loud,
Who's at the door?
I've been two weeks or more
Working up to a prayer
And now somebody's knocking.

It's Beth Ellen.
What in the world does she want?
Never see her for months at a time
And then there she is wanting something.
Still hasn't brought back those
Fifteen canning jars I loaned her
When the rain knocked her peaches off
All at once that day.
And she never even called up to say
Thanks the time I hurried over
With the ice cubes
When she'd had all those teeth out.

Why should I answer it?
It's not as if she comes over
Just to visit ever.
It's not as if she likes me.

There, she's turning away.
Good.

Well, Heavenly Father,
You've just got to answer me.
It's not as if I bother you a lot
You know I don't.
And if I could
I'd take care of it myself and just let you be.
But I don't know how.

So here I am, Heavenly Father.
Help me—
Now!

Thoughts in the Chapel

How I will
Greet the Lord
In heaven
I do not know.

But here
With the Sabbath organ
And Sabbath bread,
Or at home
Beside my bed—
Whenever we converse,
Just Him and me
(Watching the sunset
Or the sea)
I can at least
Rehearse.

GROWTH AND SELF-DEVELOPMENT

The Growing Season

A wound in my roots
From a zealous hoe

The quick demise
Of friendly weeds

A strange new stretching
With the flow
Of nourishment
From last year's leaves.

Sun and rain
By turns appear:

Growing season
Must be here.

Independence

I would stay here
Close to roots
That fed me
Close to
Cool shelter—

Always close
I would be.

Except,
I'm afraid.

Have you seen
The pitiful
Small green
That grows
In shade?

On Going Back

Cry or threaten
Or bribe or beg

A chicken cannot
Peck its way back
Into the egg.

My Season

Seeing the tree
Beneath a baptism of snow
You may call her barren.
But is it so?
And for all your watchings
On a March night
When the twigs seem dark
And the bark
Feels cold to your hand—
Can you call her fruitless
And so leave?

She smiles.
Calm in the station
Of seasons
And in the ordination
Of sun and sap and spring.

As for me?
You turn away
Impatient with
The promises you've seen.
But—inside I fill
And pulse and flow
With the urgency of green.

I've a season
Like the tree.
And all your
Faithless doubts
Will not destroy
The rising spring
In me.

Power

When she learned that she
Didn't have to plug into
Someone or something
Like a toaster into a wall

When she learned that she
Was a windmill and had only
To raise her arms
To catch the universal whisper
And turn
       turn
          turn
She moved.

Oh, she moved
And her dance was a marvel.

Journal

Put the thought
In words
And the words in ink
In a page in a book
In a very private place
Like under a mattress.

A sacred process
Wonderful as alchemy
Is at work
Even in the dark
While you sleep
Making something better
Than history:

Understanding.

New Hands

Celia got drinking from her mother
And hitting from her father
And yelling from both
Like she got pizza crusts for breakfast.

And she took it all in
And digested it and became it
Because you are what you eat.

And her parents
Ate from the table of their parents
Who ate from the table of theirs
Back and back and back
And Celia was stuck.

But cells die
And every seven years we are new.

Celia's new heart and new hands
Set the table and stir the pot
And serve better stuff than she ever got.

The Little Trees

When she was small
She used to call
Them the little trees—
Those sapling cottonwoods
A dozen or so
On the hill above the spring.

After a day's play with cousins
She would hear her mother
Calling from the door,
"Supper's almost done—
Come a runnin'."

And she would make
Her usual request:
"Please, Ma, can I walk them
To the little trees?
I'll run right back."

"All right. Hurry along."

So she would walk her cousins
To the little trees
And wave them on.

And then—
She was the one at the door
That same door, calling,
"Time to come in now
All of you
Quick as a wink.
Tell your cousins good-bye."

"Please, Mother, can we walk them
Just to the big trees?
We'll go so fast."

She watched them
Walk their cousins
To the big trees—
Those blazing green cottonwoods
A dozen or so
On the hill above the spring.

Rooted at the door
She watched them go.
And from somewhere
A wind blew through her—
The awesome thrill
Of things that grow.

A Widening View

When my eye first opened
Behind the viewfinder,
There in closeup
Was a flower—
The only possible flower.

Who turned the lens
For the pullback?
Life, I guess.
What—
Another flower?
And another?
A field alive with flowers.
(The only possible field?)

Loss.
Delight.

Borders are forever gone.
Life is at the lens.
The view goes on
And on.

LIFE'S LITTLE LESSONS

Coaching the Universe

I shout directions
To whoever is in charge
As knowledgeably
As my own little
Backseat driver,
Age three.

The Prophet's Feast

He led us to the banquet.
He blessed the food and then
Gladly he raised his fork
And the Prophet's feast began.

We watched in awe, and still
We stand with empty plate
Sincere and hungry, testify
That the Prophet truly ate.

Getting Ready

He's always getting ready
But never quite goes.
He's always taking notes
But never quite knows.

He's touched by all the starving
But doesn't touch his wife.
His life is spent at meetings
But he never meets life.

From the Philosopher

Can it be
In this huge
Hunger to know

I try so hard to see backstage
I miss the best parts
Of the show?

Connection

Incredible
That I have spent
All these seasons
Staring upward to see

How the tree
Fits the leaf
Instead of how
The leaf fits the tree.

Words

I wanted to know
What it felt like to swear.

So one day
Away out in the back pasture where
Two horses switched
For the big flies,
I stood on a little bridge
Took a deep breath
And said every bad word
I'd ever heard.

The horse tails switched on
And on ran the unpolluted stream.

It took about a week though
To wash and rinse
My mouth clean
And I've never said those words since—

Though now I'm counting
Many another word
I should have taken
To where only horses heard.

At the Church Christmas Party

My little Johnny, who was three,
Climbed with lights in his eyes onto Santa's knee.
"And what would you like this year, my boy?
If I can I'll bring your favorite toy."

Johnny didn't even need time to think.
"I want a dolly," he said, "that will eat and drink."
Twelve parents, at least, turned to look at me
And a big man said suspiciously,

"Next year he'll want a dress or two."
I replied, "It's the father in him coming through."
"Well, that's not what some folks would say.
A kid's character's built by the way he'll play."

My little Johnny, who was three,
Climbed with lights in his eyes from Santa's knee.
And the big man grinned as he watched his son
Ask Santa Claus for a tank and a gun.

The Unwritten Poem

Sometimes
In a sitting down moment
On a day
Of stove-heating the sad-irons
And layering newspaper between
Quilts to keep us warmer
I heard my mother say,
"I wish I had time
To write a poem."
And then she would start
The potatoes.

When I was twelve
A thing happened that
Broke my heart—
A school thing I've forgotten now.
For hours I cried my humiliation
Into a handkerchief.

Next day my mother
Brought it in from ironing
That handkerchief
And gave it to me special.
"Here," she laid it in my lap.
"You've had it in happy times
And in sad.
There'll be more of both.
Keep it, and it will remind you
The better follows the bad."

She went back to ironing
And my fingers traced
The little flowers of fading blue.

I can remember other poems
She left me, too.

Too Busy

It was time
To prune the apricots.
"Only one bud
Every few inches of tree
Or they won't grow,"
Said my father.

I didn't believe him
Though
And I kept one branch
All full of flowers
For I knew
They would all
Be beautiful and bright
And big—
Ever so big.

Early one morning
In fruit time
I ran to the orchard
And beneath
The heavy-hanging
Golden crop
I harvested my apricots,
My many, many
Tiny apricots.

When it was dark
I fed them
To the cow.

I prune now.

The Grade

God does not grade
On the curve,
I'm sure of it.

But we sit around
Like high school students
In an important class
Whose teacher has drawn
On the blackboard
The tiny wedges for the A's and the E's
And the great bulge for the C's.

We sigh in veiled relief
As the person down the row messes up
Because it makes us look better
And probably means an E
For him, which is good
Because while we have
Nothing against him personally
It means an A is more
Available to us.

And we secretly sorrow
When the person in front of us
Does really well
Although we like her okay
Because there goes another good grade
Darn it, and we're looking worse and worse
And slipping further down the curve.

And God, I think
Sits at the front of the class
Holding A's enough for all
Watching us work out our salvation
In fear and competition.

For a Daughter in Love

I would not walk on her happiness
Any more than I would
Walk on a brand new lawn.
It is too tender.

I will not tell her now.

She has fallen in love
And I will wait until she has gotten up
And is standing straight.

I will wait until she comes to me
With questions in her eyes like tears.

I will tell her then
Like we finally tell the person
Who is sent out of the room
In those silly games we used to play
Tell her what everybody else
Has known, each in their turn:

That falling in love is a trap
Whereby life snatches people by the two's
And ties them so tightly together
That they can't get away
Until they learn something.
Learn about love, real love:
Being in, working in, living in
Rising in—all begun by
Falling in.

I hope she will be a good sport
And nod her head and even smile
And say,
"Okay."

FRIENDS
AND
RELATIONSHIPS

Support Group

You can fall here.
We are a quilt set to catch you
A quilt of women's hands
Threaded by pain made useful.

With generations of comfort-making
Behind us, we offer this gift
Warm as grandma's feather bed
Sweet as the Heavenly Mother's
Lullaby song.

You can fall here.
Women's hands are strong.

All Us Millions

Divided by darkness
Blended by the sun—
Through some amazing mathematics
We come out
One.

The Friend

Let me
Be the hearth
Where you sit
To work your clay.
I'll not say
"Shape it like this
Or like that,"
I promise.

Let me watch
As you
In absolute agency
Mold your
Mortal dream.

Only
Sit close
And let me give
A little light
A little warmth.
Yes
Warmth especially.

Cold clay yields
To no form.
Let me
Be your hearth.
Sit close
Be warm.

The Forgiving

Forgive?
Will I forgive,
You cry.
But
What is the gift
The favor?

You would lift
Me from
My poor place
To stand beside
The Savior.
You would have
Me see with
His eyes
Smile
And with Him
Reach out to
Salve
A sorrowing heart—
For one small
Moment
To share in
Christ's great art.

Will I forgive,
You cry.
Oh
May I—
May I?

Johnny's Shoes

He read the Johnny-sized words
And I read the big ones:

"Love your enemies
Do good to them that hate you
And pray for them
Which despitefully use you."

He knelt for evening prayer
Pure as Johnny is always pure:

"Heavenly Father,
Thank you for the good day
That we've had
And please bless the person
Who stole my shoes at the
Swimming pool today that he
Won't have to steal anymore
And that he can have more
Love inside of him. . . ."

Out the window
Or through the wall
(I wasn't quick enough to see)
Shot some small share
Of enormous wealth
Never to be stolen
Never to lose.

And somebody somewhere
Instantly wore more than
Johnny's shoes.

Unfed

We feed one another
In rations,
Serve affection
Measured to
The minimum daily
Requirement,
The very acceptable
Least—

While love
Bursts the walls
Of our larder
Wondering
Amazed
Why we are afraid
To feast.

The Waste

They're dumping wheat
Into the sea,
And oranges too
I hear.

Just like my heart
That annually
Wastes fields of love
For fear.

The Sunflower

Of course you have clouds.
What mortal sky does not?
Only in heaven
Are the heavens clear forever.

It's all right.
I am a sunflower.
I will find the light.

Prejudice

The celestial soul
Bigger than boundaries
Extends
Past labels of name
Or place or shade.

It will take
I think
A long time
To learn how.

Should we not
Start now?

The Touch

Robert reached out
And took his father's hand.
His father didn't notice.
He had been in a coma three days
And was not expected to notice things again.

Lying there, white against the white sheet,
He looked like a drawing that had been
Sketched but not colored in
Except for the mustache and eyebrows
Done with a black crayon.

"Dad—"
Robert's voice was quiet.
His voice had always been
More quiet than his father's.

"Dad—I'm here.
I'm holding your hand.
You don't mind, do you?
All last night on the airplane
That's what I was thinking about—
Getting here in time to hold your hand
And say a few things.

Can you understand?
I know you can't speak
But can you understand?
Maybe I'm talking more for me
Than for you anyway
But that's okay.

Would you mind—if you were awake—
My touching you? I want to.
Why wouldn't you ever touch me?

I've got that picture of us
On my birthday when I was three
And you were holding me on your lap.
That must have been the last time
Because except for a few spankings
And all the handshakes
You hardly ever touched me again.
You even said 'Excuse me' if we happened
To brush in the hall.

Why did you have to shake my hand, Dad?
Why couldn't you ever hug me?
One time when I was over at David's house
His dad came in and kissed him
And he wasn't even going on a trip.
I must have looked amazed, because he said,
'What's the matter, Robert—haven't you seen
A man kiss his own son before?"
I hadn't.

Do you remember that I would never go out
To a real barber, Dad?
Do you know why?
Because once a month, when you gave me
A haircut in the kitchen—you touched me.
And it felt so good.

I think I was out of high school
Before I went to a real barber.
And since then we've had only handshakes, Dad.
I was so hungry—for so long.

Didn't you ever want to say 'I love you'
To anyone, Dad?
If you said it to Mom I didn't hear you,
And if you said it to me
I was asleep—or under three.

I guess you didn't think a real man
Did things like that.
I remember once when Mom was sick
And you did the dishes for her
You pulled the blind down
So nobody would see.
And the time my best friend moved away
And I cried, you told me
To be a man about it.

Dad, I know I'm not the kind of man
You think a man ought to be.
I haven't gotten ahead like you wanted
Or made the money you thought I should.
Sometimes I cry, Dad.
And I even—Dad—I hug my little boys.
Even my big boy. And I kiss them.
It feels so good.

When you came to visit last Christmas
I wanted to put my arms around them
Right there in front of you—
But I couldn't.
And I wanted to put my arms around you—
But I couldn't.
So we shook hands and you left."

Robert stroked his father's arm.
"Dad—I used to blame you
But I don't anymore.
You did what you knew.
And I do too.

That's why I prayed all night on the plane
That I'd get here—in time to touch you
And to say—"

Robert stood and gathered the old man
In his arms and lifted him a little.

"Dad—I love you."
Then he kissed the old man's cheek
And his forehead and his lips.

Robert may have imagined it
But he thought he felt a slight, slight pressure
From the white, white fingertips.

Split

You felt safe
I know
In that little space
Laced with love.
Your cocoon
You called it
Warm
Warm.
I cried with you
When it split.

Oh, safe
Cannot compare with sky.
I like you so much better
As a butterfly.

The Lighthouse

Do you know
How many count on you
To steer by this night?

Do you know
How dark the sea
And dim the stars
And strong the wind
Out there?

And you would
Hide your lighthouse
Under a bushel?

Don't you dare!

The Days We Shared

They were generating days
The days we shared
Bright as when
Two fires combine.

I leave
Wearing some of your light
As you leave
Wearing some of mine.

Our Heart's
in the Barnyard

The senator's wife is arrested
For drunken driving
And the newsrooms tap out applause
From coast to coast.

A celebrated marriage ends
And the cameras crane to get
Close enough to catch the death
In living color.

A chicken takes sick
And a dozen friends come quick
To peck past the last
Shiver in the reddening mud.

Barnyard creatures
Have such a taste for blood.

For the Friendly Neighborhood Gossip

The children's turtle
Stayed in his shell
One day.
He's sick,
They thought.
And to see
If the poor thing
Was still alive
They got some sticks
To poke inside.

They were right.
Pretty soon
Poor turtle
Died.

The Sheep

Secure in company
Watching whosever wool
Happens to be
Up front—

The sheep gladly
Gathers his legs
And
With blissful "baa"
And unsuspicious sniff
Dives off
The cliff.

To One Who Has Been Done Dirt

Cry or curse or call it unfair
But be grateful till the grave
That in this hurt
You're the one who received
And not the one who gave.

The Nourisher

Without recipe
Without dish
You bring a banquet.

You step into a room
Open, mix, bake and serve.
Instantly the feast is spread.

Instantly
I am fed.

Let Go

When you're giving birth
Let go.

When you're watching at death
Let go.

Whenever a life needs
A life apart
Hold your heart.
Let go.

⤖ WOMEN ⤗

On Nest Building

Mud is not bad for nest building.
Mud and sticks
And a fallen feather or two will do
And require no reaching.
I could rest there, with my tiny ones
Sound for the season, at least.

But
If I may fly awhile—
If I may cut through a sunset going out
And a rainbow coming back
Color upon color sealed in my eyes—
If I may have the unboundaried skies
For my study
Clouds, cities, rivers for my rooms—
If I may search the centuries
For melody and meaning—
If I may try for the sun—

I shall come back
Bearing such beauties
Gleaned from God's and the world's very best.
I shall come filled.

And then—
Oh, the nest that I can build!

Dreams

Martha
Cleaning house
After the last child left
Finds her favorite biology text
And blows dust from the dream
She grew up with.
Is forty-eight too old
To enroll in veterinarian school?

And Georgia
Down the street
Home from board meeting
With a new pile of papers
Wryly smiles
As she pulls from the closet
The oak cradle
She had intended for something
Other than overflow
For her most important files.

Millie's Mother's Red Dress

It hung there in the closet
While she was dying, Mother's red dress
Like a gash in the row
Of dark, old clothes
She had worn away her life in.

They had called me home
And I knew when I saw her
She wasn't going to last.

When I saw the dress, I said,
"Why, Mother—how beautiful!
I've never seen it on you."

"I've never worn it," she slowly said.
"Sit down, Millie—I'd like to undo
A lesson or two before I go, if I can."

I sat by her bed
And she sighed a bigger breath
Than I thought she could hold.
"Now that I'll soon be gone
I can see some things.
Oh, I taught you good—but I taught you wrong."

"What do you mean, Mother?"

"Well—I always thought
That a good woman never takes her turn
That she's just for doing for somebody else.
Do here, do there, always keep
Everybody else's wants tended and make sure
Yours are at the bottom of the heap.

Maybe someday you'll get to them
But of course you never do.
My life was like that—doing for your dad
Doing for the boys, for your sisters, for you."

"You did—everything a mother could."

"Oh, Millie, Millie, it was no good—
For you—for him. Don't you see?
I did you the worst of wrongs.
I asked nothing—for me!

"Your father in the other room
All stirred up and staring at the walls—
When the doctor told him, he took
It bad—came to my bed and all but shook
The life right out of me. 'You can't die,
Do you hear? What'll become of me?
What'll become of me?'
It'll be hard, all right, when I go.
He can't even find the frying pan, you know.

"And you children.
I was a free ride for everybody, everywhere.
I was the first one up and the last one down
Seven days out of the week.
I always took the toast that got burned,
And the very smallest piece of pie.
I look at how some of your brothers treat their wives now,
And it makes me sick, 'cause it was me
That taught it to them. And they learned.
They learned that a woman doesn't
Even exist except to give.
Why, every single penny that I could save
Went for your clothes or your books
Even when it wasn't necessary.
Can't even remember once when I took

Myself downtown to buy something beautiful—
For me.

"Except last year when I got that red dress.
I found I had twenty dollars
That wasn't especially spoke for.
I was on my way to pay it extra on the washer.
But somehow—I came home with this big box.
Your father really gave it to me then.
'Where you going to wear a thing like that to—
Some opera or something?'
And he was right, I guess.
I've never, except in the store,
Put on that dress.

"Oh, Millie—I always thought if you take
Nothing for yourself in this world
You'd have it all in the next somehow.
I don't believe that anymore.
I think the Lord wants us to have something—
Here—and now.

"And I'm telling you, Millie, if some miracle
Could get me off this bed, you could look
For a different mother, 'cause I would be one.
Oh, I passed up my turn so long
I would hardly know how to take it.
But I'd learn, Millie.
I would learn!"

It hung there in the closet
While she was dying, Mother's red dress
Like a gash in the row
Of dark, old clothes
She had worn away her life in.

Her last words to me were these:
"Do me the honor, Millie,
Of not following in my footsteps.
Promise me that."

I promised.
She caught her breath
Then Mother took her turn
In death.

High

The high that Glenda felt
After going one more day
And one more day
Without reaching for the pills
After actually getting through
The holidays unanesthetized

Was perhaps not as intense
As the other high
But it had fringe benefits;

It did not make her lie
It did not make her husband cry
And it left her looking
At the woman in the
Medicine cabinet mirror
With a hopeful eye.

The Steward

Heber looked at his lands
And he was pleased.
He'd be leaving them tomorrow, and his hands
Hurt with anticipated idleness.
But he knew there was no other way
When a man is seventy-eight and has to make
Two rest stops with a full bucket of milk
Between the barn and the kitchen.
Condominiums—do they have gardens?
He wondered.
His son had arranged the place for them in town
And he was ready. He sat down
On the rock that knew his body
Better than the front room chair.

Could it really be fifty-five years ago
That sitting right there
They had talked?
His father's voice had never left him:
"Heber, I'm trusting to you
The most precious thing I've got.
I worked hard for this land. You know all about
The crickets and the Indians and the drought
And the buckets of sweat it took
To make what you see today.
I'm giving it to you as a stewardship, son.
And when your time with the land is done
And we get together again
I'm going to call you to account.
I'm going to say, 'Heber, did you make it more
Than you found it? Did you watch it
And tend it? Did you make it grow?
Is it everything it can be?'
That's what I'll want to know."

Heber looked out on the fields
That for fifty-five years had been
Green and gold in proper turn—
On the fences and the barns and the ditches
And the trees in careful rows.
Even his father hadn't been able to get peaches.
He could hardly wait to report about those.

Margaret was finishing the last closet.
Just a few things were going to the city
And the rest rose in a mountain
On the back porch, waiting for the children
To sort through and take what they chose.
She opened the lid on a shoebox of valentines.
Perhaps just one or two for memory's sake?
But whose—whose would she take?

She put the box aside and reached again.
"What in the world?" In an instant her face
Cleared and in her hands was the old familiar case.
The violin. She hadn't touched it for forty years
Hadn't thought of it for twenty at least.
Well, there they finally were—the tears.
Her mother's dishes hadn't done it
Or the little Bible she had almost buried with Ellen
Or the valentines—
But there they were for the violin.

She picked up the bow.
Had it always been so thin?
Perhaps her hand had grown so used to big things
To kettles that weighed ten pounds empty
And to milk cans and buckets of coal.

The wood felt smooth against her chin
As she put the bow to a string.
A slow, startled sound wavered then fell.

How did she used to tune it? Ah, well,
No sense wasting time on moving day.
If Heber should come in he would say,
"Well, there's Margaret—fiddlin' around
With her fiddle again."
He'd always said it with a smile, though.

"I could have done it," she said out loud.
"And it wouldn't have hurt him.
It wouldn't have hurt anybody!"

He hadn't minded that she'd practiced two hours
Every afternoon—after all, she got up at five
And nobody in the world could criticize
The way she kept the house
Or the care she gave to the children.
And he was proud that she was asked
To play twice a year at the church.
And music made her so happy.
If she missed a day things were not quite
So bright around the house.
Even Heber noticed that.

And then she was invited to join
The symphony in town.
Oh, to play with a real orchestra again!
In a hall with a real audience again!

"But, Margaret, isn't that too much to ask
Of a woman with children and a farm to tend?"

"Oh, Heber, I'll get up at four if I have to.
I won't let down—not a bit. I promise!"

"But I couldn't drive you in,
Not two nights a week all year round,
And more when they're performing."

"I can drive, Heber. It's only twenty miles.
I'd be fine. You would have to be
With the children, though, until Ellen
Is a little older."

"But I couldn't guarantee two nights a week—
Not with my responsibilities to the farm
And to the church."

"Heber, there's no way to tell you
How important this is to me. Please, Heber.
I'll get up at four if I have to."

But Heber said no.
What if something happened to the car?
And then it just wouldn't look right
For a man's wife to be out chasing
Around like that. What would it lead to next?
Once in a while he read of some woman
Who went so far with her fancy notions
That she up and left her family, children and all.
He couldn't see Margaret ever doing that
But it's best to play it safe.
Two nights a week—that was asking a lot.

So Heber said no.
It was his responsibility to take care of her.

She had been given to him, in fact.
He remembered the ceremony well
The pledges, the rings
And he didn't take it lightly.
She had been given to him
And it was up to him to decide these things.
So Heber said no.

She had seemed to take it all right
Though she was quieter than usual
And more and more an afternoon would pass
Without her practicing.

He didn't really notice how it happened—
The shrinking of her borders
The drying up of her green.
If Heber ever thought about it in later years
He marked it up to the twins.
Motherhood was hard on a woman
And Margaret just wasn't quite the same as before.

She laid the violin in its case
And rubbed away the small wet drop
On her thin hand.

"I could have done it," she said aloud.
"Heber, you didn't understand.
I could have done it and not hurt anybody.
I would have gotten up at four!"

Slowly she made her way to the porch
And put the violin with the things
For the children to sort through.

"Will any of them remember?
I don't think so."

Heber gave a last look at his lands
And he was pleased.
He could face his father with a clear mind.
"Here's my stewardship," he would say,
"And I think you'll find
I did everything you asked.
I took what you gave me—and I made it more."

He got up and started toward the house.
Putting to his lips
A long, thin piece of hay.
"Better get movin'. Margaret will be
Needing me for supper right away."

Ms. Mead Said So

In every tribe
No island excepted

Basket weaving
If done by men
Is not stuff
Real buff:
Masculine.

And basket weaving
If done by women
Is mere fluff
Not enough:
Feminine.

So women, of course
Are leaving their weaving

And whatever will we
Float the children in?

Laura and the Empty Tray

Sitting on the bench
Waiting for the bus
Laura looked like a person
Trying to look like the people
Who know where they're going.

Laura had been booted out of the house
By her husband
Whose last words to her had been
"I don't want to see you until five o'clock,
And don't you dare come home a minute sooner."
And then almost pleadingly
"Have a good time."

She had begged Stephen not to make her go
Not to make her spend a whole
Eight hours out there
Doing anything she wanted to do.
She was already doing what she
Wanted to do, and she didn't have
Time for anything else.

"But honey," he had said
"If there were more time
If another whole day were magically
Tossed into the week—
A day just for you—
What would you want to do?"

Laura's answer came as quickly
As the computer prints item and price
In the grocery store:
"The downstairs bathroom," she said.
There had been two cans of paint
Beside the tub for months.

White eyes staring accusingly
At the walls that were slowly peeling
And at Laura, who was running in and out
Trying not to think
About the paint and the tube of caulking
For the sink.

It was easy.
What would she do with another day?
The downstairs bathroom.

Stephen had taken her by the shoulders
And looked deep into her eyes
As if his own held a flashlight.
"Laura, where are you? Where are you?
I can't find the woman I love anymore.
She's lost. Help me find her."

Laura lowered her eyes and thought.
"Aren't we supposed to lose ourselves?
Isn't that what service is all about
Forget yourself and serve others?"

"No," he said. "It's not.
You're supposed to serve everyone
But you've been forgetting someone.
What can you serve from an empty tray?
How can you water plants from an empty pot?"

Laura started to cry.
When frustration began to well
Like the hot springs at her uncle's ranch
She always cried.
He was right. She had been going on empty
For a long time.
She had been reaching into herself
As into an apron to throw feed

To a yardful of chickens
And coming up with empty hands.
And the chickens cried louder
And sometimes she felt like wringing their necks
And sometimes like jumping over the fence
And running, running, running.

Stephen put his arms around her
And drew her close.
He hated to have her cry.
He would rather she yell or even hit.
But she always cried
And hid in some dark corner inside
That no flashlight could find
Making him stumble around in his search
Palms out for blind man's bluff.
So he took her in his arms
And Stephen cried too
Because he loved her.

"Look," he finally said
Pulling her down beside him on the couch.
"Next Wednesday will be your day.
Go out—do anything you want to.
I'll hire a babysitter and get off early—"

"Pay?" she interrupted
Looking at him like she looked at her children
When they suggested moving to Disneyland.

"A babysitter," he said quietly
"Is cheaper than a psychiatrist."
Laura began to cry again.
He was talking about Donna
A friend from where they used to live
Who they'd just learned had spent two months
In a psychiatric hospital.

How had it happened to her?
She had been the one who had done
Everything perfectly all the time
And done it with a smile—
Until she began kicking her children
And taking twice as much valium
As her doctor prescribed.

On Wednesday Laura was out of the house
By ten, telling the children
Something that was not quite a lie
And giving the babysitter the
Longest possible list of things to do.

And now, sitting on the bench
Waiting for the bus
Laura looked at her watch.
Where in the world could she go
For a whole day?
If she had the children with her
They could go to the zoo—she'd been
Promising to take them to the zoo for months.
She looked at her watch again.
What if she went back to the house
Climbed in the window downstairs
And did the bathroom?
No. Stephen would ask for a full report
And she couldn't lie.

Laura sighed, and the same feeling
Arose from the pit of her stomach
That comes with sitting in a traffic jam
When the dinner in the oven will be ruined
If it doesn't come out in fifteen minutes.

With everything she had to do—
Why—why did he make her—?

"I'll clean out my purse," she thought.
"I've been needing to clean out my purse."
Quick, efficient fingers emptied her bag
Putting the good things in one pile
And the junk in another—
Sugarless gum wrappers, old grocery lists
A petrified apple core
The arm of a Barbie doll
A program from last week's church service
And a handful of cracker crumbs.

She threw the rubbish
In a garbage can by the bench and shook
Out the empty purse.
There, that felt better.
At least she'd have something
To show for her day.
Why hadn't she brought the bills?
Stephen would never have noticed
If she'd stuffed the bills and envelopes
And stamps into her purse—she could have
Paid all the bills.

The bus arrived and Laura boarded.
Maybe downtown something would come to her.

Looking out the window, Laura filed her nails.
Good thing she always carried
Her nail file around in her purse.
Then she did the eye exercises that
Once in a while she got around to doing.
Let's see. She didn't need a haircut.
Darn—if she'd brought her lists she could have
Gone to a phone booth and made her calls
For church and for the bake sale at school.

She looked at her watch again

And figured out what the babysitter had earned.
That feeling came again from her stomach
And she watched the babysitter's fee climb
Like you watch the meter at the gas station—
Fifteen cents—twenty cents—twenty-five cents.

The hot springs began to well again.
Why is he making me do this?
The bus passed the department store.
She could go in and get underwear
For Crissy, who had only two decent pair
But Stephen had made her promise
If she bought anything it would be for her.
The bus stopped and Laura got off
And looked around
Like someone in a strange airport.
Maybe she should have saved the arm
Of the Barbie doll. Oh, well.
Let's see. She could buy some pantyhose.
That would be for her.
But if she saved the money
She wouldn't feel quite so bad about
The meter at home soaring higher and higher.

Two blocks away was the library.
Darn—why didn't she bring the book
She had found under the couch—
Bedtime for Frances.
She had paid for it already
But maybe if she brought it back anyway
They would reimburse her—do they do that?
It wouldn't hurt to ask,
She had nothing else to do.

The walk to the library felt good.
It always felt good to walk with a purpose.
She opened the heavy door and was overcome,

As she always was, with the smell of the library—
That wonderful gluey smell that instantly catapulted
Her back into the excitement of adolescence
And school and learning
And looking at who else was there.
She'd always had to back in and out
Of library doors, for her arms were always loaded.
As Laura headed toward the desk
A display of paperbacks caught her eye.
To Kill a Mockingbird.
The title jumped out at her.
Just the other night she had driven
A group of high school girls home
From a volleyball game at the church
And they had been complaining about
Having to read *To Kill a Mockingbird*
Thirty pages a day.

Laura had laughed.
"Oh, boy—I wish your English teacher
Would assign me to read
To Kill a Mockingbird.
Wouldn't I love to have to read
Thirty pages a day?"

Slowly Laura reached out and picked up the book.
A smile crept over her face and she looked around
Like you do when you find money on the ground.
Could she? Would it be okay?
Stephen made her come.
It wouldn't be her fault.

Laura chose a chair with cushions
And opened the book as guiltily
As if it had just come in the mail
In a plain brown wrapper.

At twelve o'clock she had not
Shifted once in her chair.
At one o'clock she shifted in her chair
But forgot the peanut butter sandwich
And banana in her purse.
At two o'clock she did not know that
She was in a chair—or a library—
Or a mortal body.
At 5:08 she closed the book
And stared at the wall for minutes
Stared without seeing.
Suddenly she focused on the clock and jumped.
She was supposed to be home by five!

Quickly she put the book back on display
And then ran to the pay telephone by the door.

Her fingers easily found a coin
(Good thing she had cleaned her purse)
And she dialed her number.

"Hello?"
"Oh, Stephen, I'm so sorry.
I'll be home as soon as I can.
I came to the library to see
If they would reimburse me
For *Bedtime for Frances.*
But I forgot to ask them and I—
I read a book—I read a whole book, Stephen.
Stephen—are you there?"

"Laura?"
His voice was the voice you use
With your doctor after he has studied
All the tests.
"Laura? Did you have a good time?"
"Oh, yes. Oh, Stephen, it was wonderful!

I can't wait to tell you.
Oh, Stephen, thank you!"
Laura began to cry.
And Stephen cried too
Because he loved her.

Laura had to back out of the library door
For her arms were loaded.
Some of the books were for the children
But some were for her!

She ran the two blocks to the bus
Heavy—but not with books.
Full—like a tray, like a pot
Full like a farmer's apron
And she couldn't wait to throw it all
To the little chickens
And anybody else in the yard.

She had tomorrow all figured out.
Just think!—
A bathroom wall, then a book for the children
Then a chapter for her, then a bathroom wall
Then a book for the children
Then a chapter for her.
And then, if she really felt like it—the sink.

Next to Godliness

There are cobwebs behind my washing machine.
I never see them except when I lean
Over to take out the ironing board
Or to put it away.
And then there they are—
An incriminating network, thin and grey.

One day
In a fit of pride, I said to myself
"Look here, cleanliness is next to godliness
And a mere half-hour would make the backside
Of your washing machine so clean
You could eat off it."

I ran toward the closet
For the rags and soap and mop.
But I had to pass by the bookcase on the way
And right there on top—
Oh, you know the rest.

Well
There still are cobwebs behind my washing machine.
But when I lean
Over to take out the ironing board
Or to put it away
There is a thought that consoles:

Heaven's got to be more
Than a place scrubbed clean
For a bunch of cob-webbed souls.

The Honor

At two in the morning Luana May was nearly done.
If she used up the scraps she could get one
More that looked as good as the rest of them.
She twisted the wires of the artificial green
Around the carnation and pinched it into a stem.

The other women had helped until midnight
But Luana May had sent them home.
After all, she was head of the women's committee
For the church and it just didn't seem right
To make them all stay up
So she insisted on finishing the job alone.

She flexed her fingers and began:
"This fragrant flower comes to say . . ."
She finished the last line
Took a moment to rub the back of her neck
Where the muscles hurt
Then attached the card to the final flower
With the final pin.

"If you want a job done right
Just get the ladies to do it,"
Brother Nelson had said with a grin.
"Like I always say—where would we be
If it weren't for you?"

Luana May
Missed most of the program the following day
The songs of the children
And Brother Nelson's talk.
Her husband's elbow woke her just in time
To reach out and accept the corsage.
She pulled out the card:

"This fragrant flower comes to say
How we honor you on this Mother's Day!"

She looked up at the bright young man
Holding the basket in the aisle.
"Why, thank you. Thank you very much,"
She said with a smile.

This Is Not What
Susan B. Anthony
Had in Mind

Down in the high school
Parking lot
The girls smoke
Rings around the boys.

(Twenty percent of females
Who have really
Come a long way
Light up, I read today
And sixteen percent of males.)

And over at the grade school
The children chant
About a pail of water:
"Jack fell down
And broke his crown
And Jill came tumbling after."

A Fascinating Study in Highs and Lows

Half a million people come there
Every year to see the view.
In fact, the pictures
On the postcards she had bought
Were taken from this very spot.

Her husband opened the door
And took her hand.
Rocks and sand
Found their way through
The straps of her little shoe
And the wind blew
A curl out of place.
Her finger touched her face
And felt a frown.
"Oh, dear," she said.
"It looks such a long way down."

"There are railings," he said
"And it's just a short walk.
Everyone says the view is great."
She took his arm, then faltered.
"I know," she smiled up at him.
"You go. I'll just sit here and wait."

He started to speak
But with a girlish giggle
She kissed him on the cheek
And said, "Now don't be mad
At your little wife. I've always had
This awful fear of falling.
Oh, how can I expect you to understand—
You're so brave and strong.
I'll just sit here.

You won't be long."
He turned her around.
"No. That wouldn't be any fun."
And he followed her back to the car
For they were one.

They sat together a moment
While thirty-three people passed by
Of the half a million that come there
Every year to see the sights.

"And shall we try for heaven, my love?"
"Oh, dear, you know I've always been—
           so afraid of heights!"

To All Women Everywhere

Let us sing a lullaby
To the heads of state.

They are our little boys grown up
And they have forgotten the sound
Of their mother's voice
And they need to be
Sat in the corner
Or given a good shaking.
Are they too big for that?

Then let us sing until their fingers
Fall from the fateful button
And they put the guns
And tanks back in the toy box
And remember that their mother
Told them we do not
Hurt one another.

Let us sing until they
Close their eyes
And dream a better dream.

Let us sing them to peace.

The Woman

God fashioned me
For feeding
And set me in
A hungry land.

I give—
To satisfy
The unconscious appetite
Of the unborn
And the child's
First thirsting need.

I give—
To be
Sweet sustenance
To aching man
And then
Quiet comfort
To a weary, wanting
World.

There is much
Hunger here.

Oh
Father—fill me
That I may nourish
Generously.

Picture Window

Kathleen
Who was out of control
Like a slope of oranges
After someone has taken
Ten at the bottom
Looked enviously at

Susan
Who carried her stress
As gracefully as she carried
The perfect pie
She had brought to the meeting
Last Wednesday night.

Kathleen
Who yelled at her children
Even when they were not
In danger of oncoming cars
And who slammed the door
After she told her husband
To have it his way then
And who once a week at least
Locked herself in the bathroom
And cried
Called

Susan
Who never perspired
And who taught classes called
"Toward a More Feminine You"
And who smiled all the time
And whose children
Always got awards

To ask if she could
Come over sometime
To get a little help.

Kathleen
Who was so disorganized
That she went on Thursday
Instead of Friday
Got a lot of help from

Susan
Who happened to be
Out front in curlers
And wrinkled slacks
And wild-woman eyes
Screaming at her youngest child
Who had just batted a ball
Through the picture window
That framed the lamp
With the beautiful butterflies.

MEN AND WOMEN

The Embryo

Love is no eagle
Strong amid
The heights.
It is an egg
A fertile
Fragile
Possibility.
Hold it warm
Within your wing
Beneath your breast.

Perhaps in heaven
Love can live
Self-nourished
Free.
But in this world
Where mountains fall
And east winds blow
Oh, careful—
Love is embryo.

The Valentine

I loved
The valentines we made in school.
I never cut the hearts out flat—
The two sides would never match for me.
I always folded and centered
And scissored out half a heart
That opened into perfect symmetry.
So they never had a side that was fat
And a side that was skinny.
I loved them for that.

I felt sort of nice and tidy that way
The day we saw the shape of our being one—
As if it had opened from some good design
That made two matching halves
Yours and mine.

But I find we don't stay put like paper.
We are not comfortable with glue.
Your edges have shifted, stretched
And mine have too—
But not to a pattern.
If we folded our halves up today
They would not fit.
Occasionally I itch for the scissors
I will admit.

Ah, well!
I will put away childish things—
Cut them off like braids.
We are no valentine, you and I.
We are something so alive, so moving
So growing, I can not yet
Put a name to the shape.

I only know it goes on and on and on
Pressing toward whatever border
There may somewhere be.

Your center and mine are one
And between the halves there is flow.
That is much.
I will let the edges go.

Sabbath

And you are
My Sabbath, too.

I come to you for rest,
Renewal,
Come to worship God in you
And God in me.

Silently
As light through the religious reds
And blues and gold of glass
In a cathedral window
I come to you for peace.

Haiku from a Male Chauvinist Deer

Shameless doe leaping
The fields at full speed—making
A buck of herself.

At Sea

One wrecked at sea
May die of thirst
Or die of drink.
I always thought
I would refuse
The generous cup.

But
Oh, my love—
I find a salted sip
Still holds some power
To satisfy.

I cannot choose today
To die.

From the Grammarian

Putting you
In the past tense
Was, I'm afraid
The hardest
Conjugation
I ever made.

Together

Perhaps we can be together there
In that next place
Where bodies are so pure
They pass through planets—

Perhaps there
Where the light that lighteth the sun
Is kept on all night every night
And no one watches for morning
Holding the cold off with a candle—

There, perhaps
Where pain is exchanged
For peace and a memory—

You and I can touch as we pass
And gather in the good of one another.
We can love and give
In whatever loving, giving ways
There finally are.

We still will wish
To be together then, I think.
Perhaps then we shall know how.
Perhaps, even, we shall know why
We cannot be together now.

Relegated to the Kitchen

In the front room
Grandfather and the men
Straightened ties and shoulders
Exchanged business cards
And solutions for the war
Slapped backs at jokes
And were very hungry.

And in the kitchen
Grandmother
And the aproned women
Warmed the hors d'oeuvres
And one another
Hugged, kissed cheeks
Touched each other's hair
Talked heartbreak and hope
And dreams of the day
And were filled
Before the filling
Of the first tray.

Not a Pair

Alison agreed
To become part of a couple
Not half of a pair.

A pair of skiis
Must ride the slope
Without a deviation
And if one makes
An independent motion
The jig is up.

A pair of socks
Must cling together in the wash
And if one takes a spin
With the sheets or the towels
The other sits on the shelf
Flat and waiting for its match
To show up with the next batch.

Alison had been paired before
And it scared the daylights out of her
To even think of linking up with anyone.

She had been a sock lost in the wash
Had been a ski that caused upsets on the slope
And she wasn't now about
To become a glove.
But she loved him and he loved her
And they decided "couple"
Was a word roomy enough
That they could both live in it.
It had two syllables anyway
Instead of one
And it even sounded like dancing
Which these days
Lets you be
Both together and free

All
over the hall.

After the Mastectomy

They were afraid it would be different
To make love without
Her breast on
And it was.

Right from the start
It brought him closer
To her heart.

Filling You

I want to fill my days
With filling you.

I am acres of wheat.
Let me harvest, mill
Mix, rise, bake, spread
With honey
And serve you
Breakfast in bed.

Mother and Other Child

After feeding him and the children
And picking up after him and the children
And instructing him and the children
   again how to scrape their plates

After scolding him and the children
   for fighting over the television
And pleading with him and the children
   to get their homework
   and their taxes done
And smiling at him and the children
   and saying cheerily, "Oh, Sweetheart,
   just try! I know you can do it!"

She attempted to find the word
For what she felt when he
Rolled over and reached for her breast.

He would not understand "incest."
She chose "tired."

Carla and Jim

Carla and Jim
Fell in love over a cadavar
In pre-med biology
And he joked that he
Found the liver and lost his heart
That day in the lab.

They went to movies and studied after
And ate pizza and studied during
And made out and studied before
And then grades came
And she got an "A" and he got a "B"
And he didn't look into
Her brown eyes quite the same
Anymore.

Carla is thirty-five and still single
And she glances at her
Biological clock now and then
And tries to turn off the alarm
And she stitches up
And listens to the lungs and hearts
Of other people's children.

Jim works hard in X-Ray
And goes home hassled and harried
To his four children—
The three little boys they had
And the lovely girl he married.

Position

If "A" looks up to "B"
Then by nature of the physical universe
"B" must look down on "A"
Rather like two birds
Positioned
One on a tree
And one on the ground.

Or so thought Marjorie
Who had always wanted to marry
A man she could look up to
But wondered where that
Would place her
If she did.

Imagine her astonishment
When she met Michael and found
That together they stood
Physics on its head.

You could never
Draw this on paper
For it defies design

But year after year
They lived a strange
Arrangement
That by all known laws
Could not occur:

She looked up to him
And he looked up to her.

Second Wedding

This time a woman
Not a girl

A necklace
Not a pearl

An orchard in September
Not a branch in May

Abundant with a hundred
Tumbling loves
Fruited and golden
To gift a man

She says "I do"
And knows "I can."

Double Wedding

Let's have a double wedding,
You and me
And eros and agape.

Let us post
Interchangeable notes
On bedroom wall
And refrigerator:
"Love they neighbor."

Let us hold hands
In movies
And in the hospital.

Let us kiss
Shoulders and eyelids
And the cut fingers
Of small children.

Let us serve one another
Apple blossoms in vases
And quartered fruit
On trays.

Let us write poems
And wills to each other.

Let us have nights
As friendly lovers
And days as loving friends.

And let the four of us,
You and me
And eros and agape,
Stand in line together
At the grocery store
And at a golden
Anniversary.

To One Who Waited

I could have
Come to you before.
But the fields in me
Wanted a little greening.
I needed
Just to work on spring
A little more.

Well
I did.
April blossomed into May.
And every early
Bud you glimpsed—
Look:
Each a bouquet.

To One Who Worries about Being Found

Does the flower fret
That the bee
Might forget
To buzz by?

Ah, no.
One concern
Has she
And she tends
It well:
Her own smell.

Last Touch

When she touched him for the first time
His skin was warm
And his hair was soft
And his fingers sweet
And the sun through the tall pines
Rose in invocation
On the blanket of blossoms
And he was so beautiful
And she had never seen such a smile.

When she touched him for the last time
His skin was cold
And his hair was thin
And his fingers shook
And the moon through the hospital window
Fell in benediction
On the little table
Heavy with flowers and fruit
And her tear joined his tear
At the little line
Where his smile began.

I Speak for Romantic Love

I speak for romantic love
Like I speak for democracy.

The woman who sees her husband
For the first time when her veil moves
At the wedding
May learn to love him
But there is something totalitarian there
Something unadult.

As the human brain is beyond the amoeba
As the ballot is beyond the dictate
Romantic love is beyond arrangement.

It is revolutionary, as America is.
It is the full flower of liberty
Opening of its own
All voluntary, hands freely raised
Because I, I will and I must
And I stand responsible for this great act
This wild, frontier adventure
Where I choose—
Where there is not master and slave
And buyer and bought
Where both are created equal
And equally invest and equally commit
And pledge allegiance to each other
Loving by consent of the lovers.

Yes, it is individual and inconvenient.
Yes, it is messy and experimental
And dangerous and may occasionally
Counter the common good.

But I salute the flag of lovers.
There is no going back.
The blessed, the free
Set foot on this land
Choice above all other lands
Kiss the soil
And delirious, reckless
Dare the most magnificent
Pursuit of happiness.

Radical

She could discuss issues
With the best of them
And did her part for the causes
Absolutely

But sometimes she left early
During refreshments
Or before the envelopes
Were all stamped
To go to another meeting

And her friends never guessed
She hurried home
Where
In a matter of hours

With one wonderful man
She established peace
Justice and equality
Ended hunger
And observed the triumph
of love.

Like Mistletoe

Being in love
Like mistletoe
Is marvelous to kiss under
But, like mistletoe
It cannot feed itself.

No more photosynthesis
Is here in this
Unspeakably sweet passion
Than is in these clustered leaves
And shiny berries birds like.

A guest
Such as being in love
And mistletoe
Requires a host
Something with a good
Root system
Something solid
Like sycamore, oak
Or respect.

Pulled loose
From a rooted thing
Even tied with red ribbon
And hung for the laughing
Singing celebration
Mistletoe
And being in love
Are charmed and charming
But only good, finally
For a few kisses.

Spring Is Only for Beginnings

Our love
Was a blossom
Full and faultless
On the tree.
But when the petals
Began to fall
All
You could see
Were the sad
Leaves scattered
On the ground.

You did not
Think to watch
For autumn
When the fruit
Is found.

Flaws

She was fed up
And ready to pack her bags
And might have hauled out the Samsonite
That very morning if she hadn't read
In the Sunday supplement how
Michaelangelo made the David
Out of a block of marble so flawed
That other sculptors passed it by.

So instead of leaving him a note
Telling him to go to hell
She sat in their room
In the reclining chair
Thinking up one nice thing to say
Which was that he always had clean hair
And then remembered too
That he was sweet to the kids
And that he laughed at her jokes
And that he didn't like his job
But every morning got up anyway.

And she remembered too
That she usually burned carrots
And didn't smell so great
In the mornings
And could stand to lose thirty pounds
And even her kids said
She'd forgotten how to play.

For two hours and a half
She sat there
Studying her marble
And measuring and figuring
And dreaming and sharpening her tools
For one more day.

At the Altar

The thought
Of forever
Teased my mind
Like a mountain
Through a thickly
Misted view.

But today the
Veil dissolved
To show—
Eternity
Is you.

Eve's Meditation

Trunk and leaf
Make the tree,
Body and wing
Make the bee.

Gazing at the garden
I cannot think it odd
That you and I together
Make the image of God.

MOTHERHOOD, PREGNANCY, AND BIRTH

Needed

The earth needs
Only nature.
If spring follows
Snow
If new seeds
Swell
Earth will go
On and on
Content.

I have watched
With folded hands
An uneasy guest.

But now
Suddenly
I am nature.
And I am needed
As all tomorrow's
Orchards
Need the present
Tree.

How good—
This nine-month
Indispensability.

The Ninth Month

Being a duplex
I have been happy, my dear
To loan you half the house
Rent-free and furnished
As best I could.

You have been a good
Tenant, all in all
Quiet, yet comfortably there
Tapping friendly on the wall.

But I hear
You have outgrown the place
And are packing up to move.
Well, I will miss
The sweet proximity.
But we will keep in touch.
There are bonds, my dear
That reach beyond a block
Or a mile or a hemisphere
Born of much love and labor.

I approve the move
And gladly turn from landlady
To neighbor.

Investment

How enviously
I watched
The rose bush
Bear her bud—
Such an easy
Lovely birth.
And
At that moment
I wished
The sweet myth
Were true—
That I could
Pluck you
My child
From some
Green vine.

But now
As you breathe
Through flesh
That was mine
(Gently in the small circle
Of my arms)
I see
The wisdom
Of investment.

The easy gift
Is easy to forget.
But what is bought
With coin of pain
Is dearly kept.

Child Making

She knew that if she had to
Hand-make this child

She would probably end up
With something like
The dress with the huge arm holes
She hid half finished
In the bottom drawer

Or the plaque on the kitchen wall
From which beans and corn
Kept dropping:

A child
With far too much skin
Or eyebrows
That just would not stay on.

So she lay back
And day after day
Knitted away
On little booties
      (uneven but sweet)

Glad she had help
In making the feet.

Matriarchal Blessing

I have blessed you
You know

Not hands on head
But body around body
Nine months encircled
By the liquid sound
Of my light

Uttering not promises
But miracles cell by cell

Giving not admonitions
But affirmations of your
Natural splendor.

You wear
You are my blessing
A blessing I author
By the power of the holy
That I bear
And that I share
By love ordained
And through which I
Pronounce you
Blessed forever.

Don's Daughter

I celebrate the birth
Of this girl child
With the joy
Of a Hebrew celebrating
The birth of a boy.

With tambourines
Or cards or calls
Her birth
Is worth
Celebrating:

See how her mother smiles
(Though that is no surprise)
But, oh
See how her father
Kneels at the cradle
Of this little goddess
With worship in his eyes!

Day-old Child

My day-old child lay in my arms.
With my lips against his ear
I whispered strongly, "How I wish—
I wish that you could hear.

"I've a hundred wonderful things to say
(A tiny cough and a nod)
Hurry, hurry, hurry and grow
So I can tell you about God."

My day-old baby's mouth was still
And my words only tickled his ear.
But a kind of a light passed through his eyes
And I saw this thought appear:

"How I wish I had a voice and words;
I've a hundred things to say.
Before I forget I'd tell you of God—
I left Him yesterday."

New Child

I savor
This mutual feast:

You
At my breast
Desperately
Drinking life

And me
Watching
Touching
Sipping eagerly
On your sweet
Evidence
Of immortality.

ADOPTION

To an Adopted

I
Did not plant you,
True.
But when
The season is done—
When the alternate
Prayers for sun
And for rain
Are counted—
When the pain
Of weeding
And the pride
Of watching
Are through—

Then
I will hold you
High,
A shining sheaf
Above the thousand
Seeds grown wild.

Not my planting,
But by heaven
My harvest—
My own child.

On Purpose

The little girl unfrowned and then
Sort of smiled when
After hearing the dictionary definition

She was told that what adopted
Really meant was

Searched for
Prayed for
Worked for
Finally gratefully got
Unquestionably on purpose
And loved a lot.

PARENTHOOD
AND
CHILD-RAISING

The Weaning

There is cloth now
Between you
And my breast—
Cloth
And a little pain.

This is the beginning.
I take your face
In my hands
And guide your gaze
Away, out there
To the fruit trees
To the stars.

My arms
Though empty
Fold comfort
To a mother-heart
That yearns for nursing
Yet knows that weaning
Is the bigger part.

Diapering at 4:00 A.M.

I saw a calf born once.
It really was amazing
How soon (all tidied up by tongue)
He wobbled off
And the new mother
Went back to grazing.

But you, my little creature
At the top of the animal kingdom
You would lie in the pasture for months
And wave your fists and cry.

So here we are,
You and I
Tied together in all
The bathings and the dryings
The pickings up and the puttings down
And the turnings over
The dressings and the undressings
And the powderings and the feedings
And the cleanings up of the comings out.

I know—
I know what it's all about
This disguised blessing of unavoidable touch
Spinning a thousand threads
That encircle us like little lariats.
And before you know it
We're caught.

Calves come for going.
But not—not my little ones.
The Lord thought it all up
This essential intimacy
And he called it good.

He created the heavens and the earth
And the seas, and the naked, needing
Infants crying to be held.
He thought it all up
This clever stratagem.

And yet—
I'll bet he smiled
When he thought about diapering at 4:00 A.M.

Bankers

He works at the bank
And has a large desk
And people listen when he talks.

And he takes good care
Of his charges:
Money, certificates
Stocks.

And she stays home
Unnoticed
And every day
Tends treasures
That outshine all the gold
In Fort Knox.

Mother to Child

Look—
Your little fist
Fits mine
Like the pit
In a plum.

One day
And one size
These two hands will
Clasp companionably.

Help me, child.
Forgive me
When I fail you.
I'm your mother
True
But in the end
Merely an older equal
Doing her faltering best
For a dear
Small friend.

Protection

Take my hand
Child—
There are dangers
At our feet.

I grope
The uneven ground
Through mist
Fearfully and slow.
But you—
(Oh, take my hand)
You go
With unsuspicious eyes
With trusting walk.

There are dangers
At our feet
And I see them all.

Take my hand
Child—
Lest I fall.

Misunderstood

Ever since I
A mere mortal mother
Learned that there was
A better way than paddling
Pinching, and pulling the ears—

I do believe
That God, grieved
By an erring daughter
Or a rebellious son
Might use a variety of
Child guidance techniques.

But vengeance
Is not one.

Child-Raising Seminar

Under the tent at the state fair
Two hundred people
Stood smiling and cheering
As the new-born calf
On little stick feet
Jacked himself inches up
And tumbled to the sawdust
And then
      blinking
           wobbling
Tried again
    and again
        and again.

And when he was finally up
All feet on the floor
The cheers became a roar

And I went home
And practiced
Smiling and clapping
for my own stumbling four.

The Vow

How could I hide you
From hate?
I would
Though my arms break
With the trying.

Life leans in
At the window there
With its bag
Of dark treasures
Trying for your eyes
So utterly open
So unaware.

You will see
Men smile over blood
And you will know
There is hate.
You may see bombs
And butcheries
And you will know
There is horror.

Against all this
What can I do?
Only vow
That before you
Leave my arms
You will know
Past ever doubting
That there is
Love, too.

The Inheritance

At the funeral my friend said to me
"What hurts most is that
Mother was always sad.
I think now
A mother owes it to her children
Just to be happy.
She never was."

Her sad face
Looked at the sad face backed by velvet.

Last time I saw my friend
Now a year since
The eyes were dry
But the face was pinched
As then and anxious hands worked
The buttons of her little girl's coat.

"I can't stay."
(She never did.)
"Jim's working tonight—as always—
But at last he got a raise.
Won't go far with the baby coming, though
And we'll have to find a bigger place.
So tired and depressed all the time.
I don't know—
Guess we'll manage—
But kids seem to need so much."

We talked a while.
Then—
"Have to go—so much to do."
I watched her rise
And do the buttons of their coats
And sigh.

A little wide-eyed girl watched, too.

The Scholar

He knew Abraham
Isaac and Jacob
Like a fellow
Tent-dweller.
He had chronicled
Their lives
Their very thoughts.

And he knew
His own son
Like the stranger
Who is given shelter
For the night
And bread
To help him on
His lost way.

He knew tears
Finally, too
Bitter and burning
When he saw how
Huge a gift
He had traded
For a pot of
Learning.

To a Child Gone

I thought I was ahead of you in line.
You would take your turn
After I took mine
Like we did before.

I guess you don't need new shoes
For starting heaven
Or a light left on against the dark
The way I always did.
But I'm so used to parenting.
I wanted just to be there
To do whatever needed to be done.

But you went first.
And now, my little one
Suddenly you are my senior.
Morning, I know, will come.
But bring close your light—
This time it is I who fear the night.

Prayer for an Afflicted Child

And now that I have fully
Informed you of her needs
Have written out the remedy
As doctor to pharmacist—
I have remembered.

I am an apprentice
Instructing the master.
Forgive me.
I will take the prescription
That you sign.

She was your child
I have remembered
Before she was mine.

For a Flawed Child

I would retouch you
Like a photograph
If I could
Smooth you and tint you
Into glossy perfection.

But we are
Without a lab, my love
And maybe I wouldn't
Do it anyway.

Some people get stuck
On surfaces, you know
So satisfied
With the outside
So thrilled with
The topmost layer of skin
They're never moved
To move within.

I have glimpsed
What's in you, my darling
And I wouldn't have you
Or anybody else
Miss it for anything.

Motherload

Motherhood has ruined me for life.

I want to nurse the world
A continent to a breast.

I want to cut up waffles
For all the third world
Send the dictator to his room
Ground the drug dealers
Wash out the pornographers'
Mouths with soap
And spray organized crime
With Black Flag.

I want to make all the politicians
And all the executives sit on the couch
And memorize the golden rule
And stand up and say it in unison.

I want to grab a bullhorn
And announce to the world
That the barbecues will stop
Until all the litter—all the litter—
Has been picked up.

Oh, I could fix everything
If they would all just listen to me
Listen to me
Listen to me!

I have such illusions of grandeur:
I am a mother.

Aaron's Other Woman

Clearly it takes
Two generations of women
To civilize a man.

I took him past
Throwing food on the floor
Peeing in public places
Saying bad words
Spitting on the sidewalk
And playing on the escalators.

But I could never
In a million mother years
Take him the quantum leap
This seventeen year-old girl
With the wispy telephone voice
And the lavender eyelids
Has taken him in one week:

Taken him by a slim
And braceleted arm
Past belching, grunting
Scowling, snapping

And into smiling, sweetness
Singing
And infinite charm.

Mother's Post Pledge

Look
I hereby:

Cross out my critique
        of your performance
Toss out my agenda
        for your life
Tear up my list of
        things you need to do
Swear up and down
        I will not do it again.

Of course it's odd
But for a while there
I mistook myself for God.

Don't Push

The minute the doctor said "push"
I did, and I've got to stop now
Because you're eighteen.

Breathe deeply
Think of something else
Don't push
Don't push.

John Leaves Home

Surely you're not going without me?
Surely you're not taking your stereo
And leaving your mother?
Surely, John, a policeman will find you
And bring you home.
We're not finished!

I read to you *The Little Red Hen*
And talked about industry.
I read to you *Animal Farm*
And talked about equality.
But I have not read to you yet
Les Miserables
Or the complete works of Shakespeare
And if I don't
Who will?

I have discussed with you at the dinner table
My hundreds of news clippings
On American-Russian relations
Acts of heroism or horror
The birth of a panda
And Ann Landers' columns on
Drug abuse, sending thank you notes
And teenage pregnancy.
But next month and the next
Newspapers will come out
And if I don't scour them for things
You need to know about
Who will?

I have made you turn off the TV
Left a list of important things to be done
In your blue color-coded notebook
On the kitchen counter:

"Mow lawn, sweep back deck, vacuum bedroom,
Write letter to grandparents, get haircut."
But the days will continue to come
With their twenty-four hours
And if I do not write out for you
A list of important things to do
Who will?

Ah, you are laughing.

Oh, John, take me with you.
Tuck a little mother in your head
And every now and then let her speak.

Take me with you.
You need to cease being a child
But I need always to be a mother
And if you won't let me
Who will?

Obedient Girl

Everybody was proud of this little girl.
She loved to please and obey.
She got good grades
And she baked good cakes
And she cleaned her room each day

(And she came home pregnant at seventeen).

She loved to please and obey.

To My Teenager

What do I do with a child
Who is taller than I?

How quickly you passed
My navel, my shoulder
My chin, my nose.
And now there is
No more of me
To measure you by.
You are off the chart
And it has thrown things
All askew.

How do you look up
To tell a person
What to do?

You can look down
And say
"Hey, the radio
Goes off now."

Height
Means "Now hear this!"
At least pulpits
And stands and stages
Assist in underlining
Amplifying
And being taken seriously.

I have lost my pulpit.
How can I preside?
Future shock is in my eyes
As I look up
And ask if you
Would be willing to
Turn down the radio
Please?

Path of a Parent

It starts with
Meditation on the toes of a baby
And leads to spiritual exercise
That would break the best yogi
Sitting cross-legged before his lotus:

Serenity
And colic
And three hours sleep last night

Grace
And the puppy feces
On the new carpet

Charity
And screams
In the grocery store when the
Oreos are ripped from white knuckles

Harmony
And three Halloween costumes
By tomorrow morning:
A clown, a witch
And a washing machine
To go with Stacey's dryer.

Honor
And another conference
With the teacher
And possibly the principal

Silence
And the roar of motorbike
And rock
And tap shoes on kitchen tile

Acceptance
And all that is dear
Packing up and leaving home

Path to god-consciousness
All begun by
Meditation on the toes of a baby.

From the Mother
of the Bride

A new family is built
Upon the ruins of the old.
The archeology is clear
And the comfort is cold.

With history as teacher
I turn accepting eyes
On the dissolving of my house—
So that yours may rise.

Wrong, Right?

You are clearly wrong
And I am clearly right.

But I will support
Your being wrong
Which is clearly the right
Thing for me to do.

Because after all
Being wrong may be
Right for you
And it would be
Wrong of me
To make you right.

So be wrong as long
As you want to.

It's quite all right.

For Children Grown and Gone

My garden could not contain
The beauty of you.

I watched you blossom
Then burst into blessings
Seeds winging in the wind
Beyond my field.

Only God can measure the yield
Or knows
All the places where
Your beauty grows.

The Mother the Harbor

These little boats
Came by currents
I may never know
From oceans I cannot see
Even from my highest hill.

I cherish the cargo
Bless the sea
And thank the eternal itinerary
That harbored them awhile
In me.

Parent Friends

There will come a time
When these little ones
That come to me now
For Band-aids and sandwiches
Will not need a mother much.
Already they are done with my womb
And done with my breast.

They will always need the rest
Of me, I believe—arms, heart, mind.
But someday I expect to find
That we walk with matching stride
And talk of things
That friends talk of.

Will there come a time
Sometime after time is done
Sometime when I no longer come to you
Dear Father and Mother
For Band-aids and sandwiches,
Will there come a time
When we walk with matching stride
And speak our common, godly concerns?

Sometime, when this infancy ends
Can we be
Not only parent and child
But friends?

～ADVERSITY～

Instructions upon Admission to Mortality

Life is a labor table
From which no one rises alive.
There is peace, even pleasure
Then pain, spaced for surprise.

Work with it, not against it.
It may help to hold the hand
Of a friend
Or to turn up the music.
Take nothing for a quick and easy end.

You are the bearer
And you are the born.
Carefully—reverently
Approach that ultimate
Delivery.

Compensation

Enormous grief
Has leveled me
Welded its bulk
To my back
And will not let
Me rise.

Yet
"I'll give
No burden that
You cannot bear"
He promised me.

I am amazed
How strong my back
Must be.

Trial Number Five

Carefully they laid
Out on the table
Trials one, two, three,
Four, five, and six.

"Choose one," they said.

"Oh, any," she cried, with a horror
Born of the best of Halloweens,
"Any but number five.
It would kill me.
I promise you I would not survive."

They thanked her graciously,
Escorted her out,
Then gift-wrapped, addressed,
And labeled "Special delivery"
Trial number five—

Sent with love from
Those whose assignment it is
To make sure you know
That you can go
Through trials one, two,
Three, four, ninety-nine,
Or five—
And, incredibly,
Come out alive.

Short Roots

The tree
At the church next door to me
Turned up its roots and died.
They had tried
To brace its leaning
But it lowered
And lowered
And then there it lay—
Leaves in grass
And matted roots in air
Like a loafer on a summer day.

"Look there"
Said the gardener
"Short roots—all the growth went up—
Big branches—short roots."

"How come?" I asked.

"Too much water.
This tree had it too good.
It never had to hunt for drink."

Especially in thirsty times
My memory steps outside
And looks at the tree
At the church next door to me
That turned up its roots and died.

Acclimated

Can you become
Acclimated to pain?
Can the shiver cease
And some condition
Almost comfortable set in?

The polar bear has been
So long a resident of frost
That the ice he walks barefoot
Is not reported to the brain.

Can you become
Acclimated to pain?

Pain

There comes a point
When pain shorts out.

An overloaded circuit takes
On charge after charge
Until
It brakes, shudders
And is mercifully
Still.

Time for the Gulls

It's time, Father
For the gulls, I think.

My arms shake
From flailing my field.
I sink
Broken as the little stalks
Beneath their devouring burden.

I yield it all to you
Who alone can touch all things.
It's time, Father
For the gulls.

I will be still
And listen for their wings.

Forgetting

Why must all memories
Stay on?

Why can't some go
In quick eclipse
Like a shooting star—
And beautifully
Be gone?

Good Ground

I have seen love
Fallen on unbroken ground
Blow with the first wind.

I have seen love
Laid in a shallow row
Unearthed with the lightest rain.

But pain
Is a plow
That opens earth for planting.

My heart is ready now.
Hurt-furrowed, it has depths
Designed for sowing.

Oh, love that lands here
Finds good ground for growing.

The Pearl

The little grain of sand
Is planted
And an ancient urge
Begins its work.

I, the unhappy oyster
Settle in the sea and curl
Defensive lustre after lustre
Around the pain—
Reluctantly
Pregnant with pearl.

Empathy

I
Since split open
Cannot contain.

I pour out
At the slightest
Sight of pain.

Miracle

To the unseen angel
Who holds to my breathing soul
The blessed anesthesia
Much thanks.

I sense the surgery
But do not feel it.
Stay close
Until time can heal it.

A Drama in Two Acts

I dim
I dim
I have no doubt
If someone blew
I would go out.

I did not.
I must be brighter
Than I thought.

SERVICE

He Who Would Be Chief among You

And he rose from supper
Poured water in a basin
And washed the disciples' feet.

Those hands
Hardened by the heat of a desert sun
Comfortable with cutting trees
And turning them to tables
In Joseph's shop—

Those hands
That with a wave could stop
The troubled sea
Could touch a leper clean,
Or triumphantly turn death away
From the loved daughter on Jairus' couch—

Those hands
That could gesture the heavens open—
Poured water in a basin
And washed the disciples' feet.

The lesson lies unlearned
But to a few
Who trust the paradox
And hear the call:

"He who would be chief among you,
Let him be the servant of all."

Giving

I love giving blood.
Sometimes I walk in
Off the street
When no one has even asked
And roll up my sleeve.

I love lying on the table
Watching my blood flow
Through the scarlet tube
To fill the little bag
That bears no address.

I love the mystery
Of its destination.
It runs as easily
To child or woman or man
Black or white
Californian or Asian
Methodist, Mormon
Moslem or Jew.

Rain does too.
Rivers do.
I think God does.
We do not.

Our suspicious egos clot
On the journey
From "Us" to "Them."

So I give blood
To practice flowing
Never knowing
Where it's going.
And glad.

Service

Who casts bread upon
The waters in crumbs
Receives it back
In loaves.

And who casts
The bread in loaves
Receives it back
In banquets.

HEALING
AND
COMFORT

The Healing

A bird
Once broken
Can never fly
They say
Quite so high
Again.

Perhaps.

But as for me
Now desperately
In need of mending
I have a healer
Who would restore
These foolish wings
Without a scar.

I will lie quiet
Beneath His touch.
I will listen
As He whispers
"Rise
And fall no more."

And then—
Then I shall
Soar.

To Be Repeated Aloud on a Discouraging Day

God
The perfect appraiser
Passed all creatures
In review
And called each good—
Including you.

Blessing

Spirit hands are on my head—
Father, Mother blessing me.
Comfort courses down like rain
Cleansing and caressing me.

Purification

If the sea
And the sun
Can bleach a bone
Till it's whiter
Than a gull
Cleaner than foam—

Oh, how bright
My soul
Can emerge
Purged
On the beach
Of Christ's water
And light.

And—

How calm
And warm
His sand.

Homemade

Woven on the little loom
Locked inside the inside room
Spun to size without a seam
Just the weight of last night's dream
A shield against this morning's night
Homemade, perfect—a garment of light.

The Laying On of Hands

Galaxies whirl within.
Little lightnings of love
Charge down arms
Out palms.

A birthing is begun:
Warmth, sight
And a gentle, private
Rising of the sun.

Christ Children

Let us make you a child again
For Christmas.
Let us put you in the cradle
As we put Jesus in the manger
Pre-crucifixion and sweet
With just-born eyes that meet
The wonder of star and smile.

For a little while
Let us make you children again.
Here there are no nails
In your innocence.
Here there is over you
A sky bursting bright
And under you the breast of a mother
Softer than hay.

You will not stay
I know
And Jesus will have to go
To Golgotha:
His little hands were born
To bear a cross.
And you, my darling
Came to the same sad world
Where trust is lost
At the hands of those who
Know not what they do.

At the end of the story
The Christ will rise
And so will you.

But let us make you
Children again for Christmas
(The Christ children that you are)
Touched only by swaddling
And the light of a star.

OLD AGE

Still Life

The first thing she did
When she walked in the door
After the doctor talked about
Six months if she was lucky

Before she read the leaflet
Clutched in her hand on chemotherapy

Before she called her sister

Before she sat on the couch and stared

She went to the back closet
And upwrapped the easel
And the oils that were still good
Which the children had given her
Several Christmases ago.

And set them up in the kitchen
Where the afternoon light hit
Her little garden in a pot
Her little African violet.
She studied the seven purple flowers
With five golden knots
As though embroidered at each center.
She studied the thirteen green velvet leaves
And the underside where the vulnerable
Red veins ran.
She had never seen anything more beautiful

And she began.

To an Aged Parent

"Here, Dad—
Let's tuck in the napkin
Just in case."

    The spoon makes its
    Hazardous trip to your mouth
    And you glance at my face
    To see if I notice.

"All clean?
Grab hold then—up you come."

    I dry your body from the bath
    And tell of things I saw downtown
    To turn your mind from modesty.

"Now, if you need something
Just ring the bell.
I'll leave the door a little open
And turn on the hall light.
Good night."

    You close your eyes
    And curl into privacy
    Free from the indignities of the day.
    "Sister, don't ever grow old"
    You used to say.
    And here you are.

    Oh, Daddy, Daddy—
    There's no way to stop it
    Or to slow it.
    Let's just let it be.

Time's strange circle
Has brought around your turn
To be comforted and cleaned
And nursed.
Shhhhhh—It's all right.
Let me hold you warm
In your last days
As you did me in my first.

Woman Aging

All her life she had been
A vegetable garden
Every inch rowed and planted
In corn, beans, carrots:
Producing
Nourishing
Doing.

Now some landscape architect
Has rearranged the space
Clearing, softening
Putting in a little pond
And a path and sand
Offering a quiet place
For being
For sitting on the one rock
And studying
The single lotus.

Pastel and thin
She is an Oriental meditation garden
Designed for going within.

DEATH AND
BEYOND

Alone

This is how I will die—
Alone
Like I am alone here on the beach.
Those who love me will stand back
Out of the wind
While I catch the current
That rarely takes more than
One at a time
And go.

I will come here
Every now and then.
I will stand on this spot
Silent, blown.
I will practice being alone.

Death

Death is the great forget, they said
A mindless, restful leaving
Of all consciousness and care
In a vast unweaving.

And so I waited, cramped and still
For approaching Death to bring
Forgetfulness—but all he brought
Was a huge remembering.

Of Places Far

To me Istanbul
Was only a name
Until a picture
You took
Of the Blue Mosque
Came.

I don't receive
Postcards from heaven
Showing Saint Peter
At prayer
But, oh—that place
Is real enough
Now that
You are there.

The Night

Grief
Is a narrow thing
Tight against
My breath—
Begging an answer
To unanswerable
Death.

I'm remembering
A sunrise.
I saw the bright
Quick streams of light
Sing gold across
The sky.
And it came to me then
How essential
Is the night:
For only from dark
Do we know dawn
At all.

The memory lets
One small solace in.
If we must
Endure an end
To know the endless—
Oh, gladly
I will let you go:
That when I see you
Standing at the door
To that more
Permanent place
How quickly
I'll recognize
The eternal
In your embrace.

On Scott's Death

Another treasure
Has been transferred
To some foreign bank
And I didn't even
Sign for it.

Withdrawals
Exceed deposits
And what am I to do?

Tellers,
I am at your mercy.
Somewhere between here
And poverty
Pay me to the order of.

Checked
Stamped
Cashed
And then—

I shall be rich again!

Point of View

Sun and mountain meet.
"Look," I say.
"Sunset!"

But I forget
That far away
An islander
Wipes morning
From his eyes
And watches
The same sun
Rise.

What's birth?
And death?
What's near
Or far?
It all depends
On where you are.

God Speaks

Death is ugly?
Oh, my children,
No.

If you knew
The beauty
That begins where
Your sight fails
You would run
Run, run
And leap
With open arms
Into eternity.

But sad
Is a harvest
Of green wheat.

And
So you would
Feverishly
Cling to earth
And finish
Your mortal task
I merely gave
Death
An ugly mask.

Conversation with a Gentleman in Jerusalem

"I'm here to build a hotel," he said,
As we sat on a bench by the Garden Tomb.
"Right up on top of the Mount of Olives.
        Five hundred rooms."

"On top of the Mount of Olives?" I asked.
"Why, sure—best spot I ever saw.
Fact, I'm surprised that no one's beat me
        To the draw.

"We'll have picture postcards in every desk
With a glued-on piece of an olive tree—
To prove to the folks that you practically slept
        In Gethsemane."

"Uh—there's just one thing that worries me"
I said to the man. "Could you explain
What happens when the Mount of Olives
        Is cleft in twain?"

"Cleft in what?" He looked at me
As blank as the blue Jerusalem sky.
"It's not going to cleft. Well, I'd just like
        To see it try."

Before he left he examined the tomb
Memorized size and shape. I guess
The only thing he didn't see was its
        Amazing emptiness.

Vital Signs

How presumptuous we mortals are
Pronouncing one another dead
Because the eyes are closed
The lips are stilled
There is no motion in the narrow bed.

A man once came
To clear our definitions.
He knew all words, all places
All states of being
For he had traveled below all things
And above.

"Death," he said, "is darkness, is hate."
"And life," he said, "is light, is love."

Oh, look again.
A vital sign burns bright and gives
This word:

She loved, she loves, she yet will love.
And Love pronounces that she lives.

INDICES

INDEX BY TITLE

INDEX OF FIRST PHRASE

INDEX OF TOPICS AND KEY WORDS